BEYONCÉ

A Little Golden Book® Biography

By Lavaille Lavette

Illustrated by Anastasia Magloire Williams

A GOLDEN BOOK • NEW YORK

rhcbooks.com
lavettebooks.com
Educators and librarians, for a variety of teaching tools, visit us at RHTeachersLibrarians.com
Library of Congress Control Number: 2022931691
ISBN 978-0-593-56812-5 (trade) — ISBN 978-0-593-56813-2 (ebook)
Printed in the United States of America
10 9 8 7 6
First Edition

Beyoncé Giselle Knowles-Carter

is an award-winning entertainer who believes in being a positive example for others.

Beyoncé Giselle Knowles was born on September 4, 1981, in Houston, Texas. She grew up in a family of four, with her younger sister, Solange, and their mom and dad. Her father, Mathew Knowles, was a salesman. Her mother, Celestine Knowles, also known as Ms. Tina, owned a hair salon.

When Beyoncé was a young girl, she helped her mom in the salon by sweeping the floor. She saw how hard her mom worked. She watched her mom turn ideas for the salon into reality.

When Beyoncé was in elementary school, she began taking dance lessons. One day while she was dancing, her teacher began humming a song. Beyoncé started singing along, hitting every note perfectly. Amazed, her teacher encouraged her not only to dance, but to sing as well.

Beyoncé loved singing and dancing. When she was nine, she auditioned for a group called Girls Tyme. She was chosen to join the group, along with a girl named Kelly Rowland. Kelly enjoyed singing as much as Beyoncé did. The two girls quickly became best friends.

Beyoncé, Kelly, and the rest of Girls Tyme were such great performers that they competed on a television show called *Star Search*. Although they didn't win, they loved being in the spotlight, and their dreams grew even bigger.

Beyoncé's father was so impressed with Girls Tyme that he left his job to become their manager. This meant Beyoncé got to work alongside her dad while chasing her dreams.

Beyoncé, Kelly, and the rest of Girls Tyme worked hard. They practiced every day. Eventually, that work paid off. When Beyonce was fourteen, the group received an offer from a record label. The girls were going to record an album so that people everywhere could hear them sing! They were very excited, but their joy didn't last. A few months after the record deal was signed, the label dropped Girls Tyme without releasing their album.

The girls didn't let the setback stop them! They changed their group name to Destiny's Child and kept performing. They quickly got a deal with Columbia Records. A few months later, they released their first single, "No, No, No."

Beyoncé and the other members of Destiny's Child began recording more songs, touring, and doing interviews on TV. Suddenly, the group was unstoppable. They recorded another album, and in 2001, their song "Say My Name" won the Grammy Award for Best R&B Song. A Grammy is an award given for excellence in music.

Around this time, the group had a big shakeup. Two of its original members decided to leave, and new members joined the group. After some time, the girls found their groove, eventually ending up with three members: Beyoncé, Kelly, and Michelle.

Beyoncé was a young woman at that point—in her early twenties—and her dreams were coming true!

As the group's success grew, Beyoncé had opportunities to perform in new ways, including in movies. In 2002, she played a character named Foxxy Cleopatra in the movie *Austin Powers in Goldmember*. She even recorded the movie's lead single.

Performing onstage with her friends in Destiny's Child was wonderful, but Beyoncé wondered what it would be like to perform by herself as a solo artist. She decided to give it a try, and in 2003, she released her first solo album, *Dangerously in Love*.

Beyoncé's solo album included a song with a famous rap artist named Jay-Z. It was "Crazy in Love," which won a Grammy Award for Best R&B Song.

In 2004, Destiny's Child released an album called *Destiny Fulfilled*. It sold almost half a million copies in the first week! People all over the world wanted to see Beyoncé, Kelly, and Michelle sing and dance, so they went on a world tour.

Then something happened that their millions of fans did not expect—Beyoncé, Kelly, and Michelle decided to split up and focus on their own careers.

Beyoncé's second solo album, *B'Day*, was released on her twenty-fifth birthday. It featured another song with Jay-Z, called "Deja Vu."

Beyoncé and Jay-Z had become very close friends. But what started as friendship soon turned to love, and the two got married.

As a team, Beyoncé and Jay-Z could not go wrong. Not only did they make great songs, but they also had three children together—Blue Ivy, and then twins Rumi and Sir.

Beyoncé wanted to share her success with others, so in 2013, she created the BeyGOOD Foundation to help people who don't have enough to eat and to provide homes for people who don't have a place to live. The BeyGOOD Foundation's mission is to inspire people to be kind and charitable, and to be good to themselves, others, their community, and the world.

Beyoncé has won awards and recognition for her work with the BeyGOOD Foundation. And she keeps winning awards for her musical accomplishments. In 2021, Beyoncé became the most-awarded woman in Grammy Awards history, with twenty-eight wins.

"I strongly believe if you work hard, whatever you want, it will come to you. I know that's easier said than done, but keep trying."

— Beyoncé

Beyoncé continues to show the world that you can achieve success by working hard, being kind to others, and never giving up on your dreams.

Pursue your dreams— just like Beyoncé!